Black Memorabilia Around the HOUSE

Jan Lindenberger

A Handbook & Price Guide

Schiffer Publishing Ltd

77 Lower Valley Road, Atglen, PA 19310

Bisque figurine of a baby coming out of egg.
1900s. $100-125.

Designed by Bonnie Hensley

Copyright © 1993 by Jan Lindenberger.
Library of Congress Catalog Number:
  92-63106.

Printed in the United States of America.
ISBN: 0-88740-487-1

Title page photo: Composition figure of a
boy, store stimulator. 17". 1900-1920. $5,000-
6,000.

Opposite page: Ceramic figurine of an
elephant with a native man on its back and
tigers attacking. Spear missing. 22" x 16".
$250-300.

Published by Schiffer Publishing, Ltd.
77 Lower Valley Road
Atglen, PA 19310
Please write for a free catalog.
This book may be purchased from the publisher.
Please include $2.95 postage.
Try your bookstore first.

We are interested in hearing from authors
with book ideas on related subjects.

Acknowledgements

I wish to thank the following people for their help and for sharing their wonderful collections with me. My gratitude goes especially to Rose Fontanello for her hospitality and for sharing the knowledge of her vast collection. My apologies and thanks also go to the folks that I may have missed.

Lightle Antiques, Bakersfield, California
Marci Carvalho, Berkeley, California
Kari Anderson, Beverly Hills, California
Kelley's Collectibles, Desert Hot Springs, California
Truly Treasures, Dublin, California
Dixie's Southern Comfort Co-op, Elk Grove, California
Rykken & Scull, Mill Valley, California
Terri Andrus, Roseville, California
Ed Sherman, Sacramento, California
Little Red House Antiques, Sacramento, California
Sacramento's Antique Center, Sacramento, California
Lavon's Antiques, Simla, Colorado

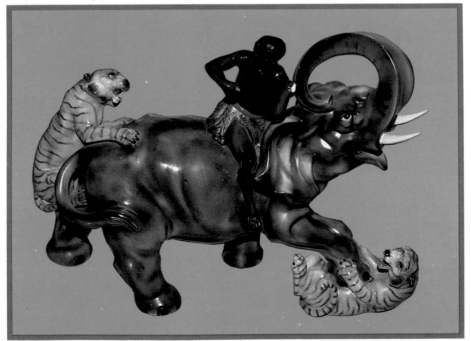

Black By Popular Demand, Jan Lindenberger, Colorado Springs, Colorado
Lewis/Blalock Collection, Washington, D.C.
Webbs Antique Mall, Centerville, Indiana
Shadeland Antique Mall, Indianapolis, Indiana
Jeanette Carson, Hyattsville, Maryland
Roger Lewis, Silver Springs, Maryland
Boone Village Antique Mall, Boonville, Missouri
Rose Fontanello, Brooklyn, New York
Leonard Davis, New York, New York
Ye Olde Canal Antiques, Milan, Ohio
North/South Antiques, Dublin, Ohio
Paradise Found, Jenks, Oklahoma
Ada Antique Mall, Ada, Oklahoma
Donna Brunello, Lafayette, Oregon
R. Malsom, Portland, Oregon
Hotel Lincoln Antiques, Manns Choice, Pennsylvania
Azle Antique Mall, Azle, Texas
Burleson Antique Mall, Burleson, Texas
Red Lane Antiques, Powhatan, Virginia

Wall clock featuring mammy holding clock.
Redwing Pottery Co. "Master Crafters" on
clock face. 10". 1940s. $300-350.

Contents

Plaster pair of native hunter and woman figurines. 24" tall. $150-200 each.

Introduction

What exactly is "black memorabilia"? To some, it is anything associated with the black people, from derogatory items to souvenirs to fine art. To others it is folk art made by black people. For others it's comprised of slave documents to shackles or anything related to the slave era. For me, it is all of this combined.

In the area of ethnic collectibles, the African-American collectible is far more broadened than any other. When was the last time you saw a Mexican salt and pepper shaker or a German head cookie jar or a Japanese yard man?

In a Wall Street Journal article that ran on August 10, 1992, Jeanette Carson (a promoter of black memorabilia shows) was quoted as saying that "of the 30,000 collectors of black memorabilia the majority are themselves black." This is their way of preserving their black heritage and to educate their children to the way things used to be in America and the way some folks perceived the black folk.

The "stereotypical" or "negative image" items seem to be the most highly collected by the black people. This may be due to the Civil Rights Act passed in 1964, "making it illegal to mass produce stereotypes". This law also made all such black items a "hot" commodity.

Some of these things were large lipped figures, rotund mammy's, or items relating to cleaning jobs. One example of this was the box of "Gold Dust Soap Powder" depicting twin black boys. This box made the statement that your clothes could become whiter by using this soap. Another was an ash tray with the jaws of an alligator wide open, ready to eat a black child. It was a popular myth that alligators liked the taste of brown flesh.

Set of seven native figurines made from nuts and wood. 4"x 1". 1940s. $100-120.

In the mid-1950s, when the Civil Rights movement began, these items began disappearing from the stores. However, many pieces are being reproduced in Japan, England, and Taiwan, including a product such as the "Darkie Tooth Paste." Pocket mirrors, Aunt Jemima buttons, cookie jars, salt and pepper sets and bisque outhouse figurines can all be ordered wholesale now. The reproduction market is growing as the older items get harder to find. Some of these items are very collectible, such as the new limited editions of the better cookie jars. Many collectors do not mind a new item as long as it's a positive image.

Which items of black memorabilia you collect is all a matter of taste. I personally love it all, but I tend to lean toward the kitchen items. (The smiling mammies in my kitchen, brighten my day.)

Several books about black memorabilia have already been written, and still all areas on this subject have not been covered. This is my second book on black memorabilia, the first being strictly on kitchen items. Many rare items are still coming out of the closets and attics.

In this book I have tried to show you, the collector, a varied selection of black memorabilia, along with the prices they are selling for today, and the approximate date they were manufactured. I truly hope you find this book helpful in your hunting.

Prices differ from coast to coast and auction prices differ from shop prices. Prices are also affected by condition and availability.

COON CHICKEN INN

Coon Chicken Inn restaurants were in Seattle, Washington, Portland, Oregon, and Salt Lake City, Utah. The logo was copyrighted in 1925 by M.L. Graham. The large smiling face of a black porter, with a winking eye was the front of the restaurant and you entered through the teeth. It was famous from 1930s through 1940s. They closed after World War Two, approximately 1951.

The sought after Coon Chicken Inn items are the plates, menus, ash trays, napkin holders, and butter pats. These, along with silverware, place mats, reserved signs, cups and saucers, stationary, employee shirts, and take out boxes, are just a few of the items made for the restaurant. The plates were made by several different companies and are so marked on the bottom. The cups and saucers only had the color on the edges with no logo. They came in two colors tan, which is the hardest to find, and aqua.

China band, set of three. "Occupied Japan." 5½". $40-45 each.

7

MAJOLICA

Majolica is a type of pottery, glazed with tin oxide to produce a soft white color. Designs are painted on white backgrounds with metallic oxides. The name comes from the Spanish island, Majorca, where potters began exporting Majolica to Italy in the mid-1400s. Centers for producing the pottery arose throughout Italy. The word should only be used to describe Italian, tin oxide-glazed pottery. But the term is also used to refer to the elaborately molded pottery that has been chiefly made in England since the mid-1800s. However, unlike true Majolica, most of this pottery is coated with a lead glaze and is generally harder and more decorative than true majolica.

Some of the black Majolica figurines were produced in the 1800s, in countries like Germany, France, and Italy to name a few.

SOUVENIR SPOONS

Souvenir spoons were made into three different sizes. The tea spoon, demi spoon and coffee spoon. The first patent date for souvenir spoons was in 1881. This was the Niagara Falls suspension bridge spoon, patented by Myron H. Kinsley. Usually the spoons are sterling and will be marked on the back side along with the makers mark. If it is not marked it probably is not sterling. Many early black souvenir spoons were made to advertise a place or a special event organized around a product. They used several stereotypes, such as, alligators, watermelons, cotton, and possums. The boy with the torn hat, "Johnnie Griffin," who was a newspaper boy in the late 1800s, was quite frequently used on the handle of the spoon. The Frederick Douglass spoon was manufactured in 1895 by William Purdy and Leonard Peters. Most of the other black spoons were made from late 1800s through 1940s.

China plate with a painting of a baby. 8".
1960s. $60-75.

1
Advertising and Packaging

Box of "Licorice Babies" candy. "Quality, Flavor, Purity." 2" x 3". 1940-50s. $35-40.

Papier mâché advertising man with arms in the air. 35". Late 1800s. $1,200.

Container for "Solid Hed Thumb Tacks." 2". 1930-40s. $25-35.

We are Clapping for Rasch's Bakery
The Place That Treats You Right

Since 1888
Satin Finish
A.P. LITTLE INC.
ROCHESTER N.Y. U.S.A.

CHECK and DOUBLE CHECK
WIGLY CANDY CO. Inc.
USE REGISTERED
WIGLY CANDY CO. Inc.

CARTER'S
Ink Eraser
THE CARTER'S INK CO.
BOSTON, MONTREAL, NEW YORK, CHICAGO

CARTER'S
MADE IN U.S.A.
INKY RACER
FOR REMOVING INK SPOTS

FUN-TO-WASH
WASHING POWDER
MANUFACTURED ONLY BY THE HYGIENIC LABORATORIES INC.
BUFFALO, N.Y.

BIGGER HAIR
TOBACCO
CHEW OR SMOKE
B. LEIDERSDORF CO.
MILWAUKEE, WIS.

Red Cross Cotton.
From Start to Finish.

PHIL DICE

PUREST SOAP BY KERK GUILD

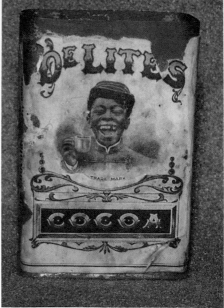

Hancock Axle grease, "Old Black Joe." Jar with lid. 1930-40s. $85-100.

Cocoa tin. "D'e Lites." 3½". Early 1900s. $75-100.

Advertising tin for Frapine malted milk. 1950s. $100-125.

Mireem Cafe au Lait Powder tin. 3½". Early 1900s. $125-150.

Left: Tin cigarette sign. "John Thomass." 1930s. $225-250. **Center:** Skuf shine shoe polish. 6½". 1940s. $60-75. **Right:** Baby bottle from the "Afro American Insurance Co. Jacksonville, FL". 8". 1950s. $75-95.

Tin match box with family watching their father point to a match holder. The text reads, "Their first box of drawing room matches, 'You chillum keep back deah! You want you heads blowed off you shoulders?'" 1½" h x 4¾" w x 2½" d. $125-150.

Aunt Sally's Lucky Dream Incense. Famous Products Co. Chicago, Ill. 1936. $45-55.

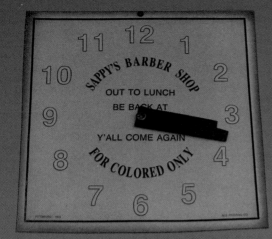

Cardboard sign for "Sappy's Barber Shop, for colored only." 1970s. $45-55.

Roly Poly Brownie tobacco tin. Opens in the center. "Dixie Queen Tobacco." 7½" x 18". $250-300.

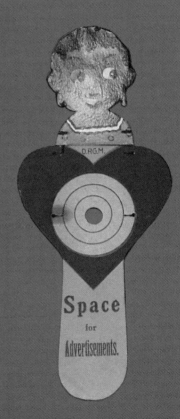

Cardboard calendar. "Hoffman Lumber Co." 1896. $90-125.

Advertising cardboard game. 9". 1920s. $50-75.

Pressed wood figure advertising "Virginia Blend." 9". 1920s-30s. $500-550.

Beer tray from Harvard Export Beer Co.
$350-400.

Advertising tray. "The source of Cottolene-
Best for shortening-Best for frying." 1920-
30s. 4½". $175-200.

"Shu Shine," plastic sign. 16" x 12". 1940s.
$75-100.

Display head of man, made of plaster. Plug in
and eyes light up. 11". 1930s. $2500-3000.

Wooden figurine, carved by Dressler,
advertising cigars. 16". $300-325.

Restaurants

Cardboard fan from "Coon Chicken Inn restaurants." 10" x 7¼". 1930-50s. $90-110.

Coon Chicken Inn food receipt. Paper. 3½" x 5½". $45-55.

Coon Chicken Inn spoon or napkin holder, 6". 1920-50s. $165-190.

Matches from Coon Chicken Inn, showing the face. The mouth was used for the entrance. 1½" x 2". $30-35.

Pot metal Coon Chicken Inn tooth pick holder of smiling porter. Small size, 3". 1920-1950. $275-300.

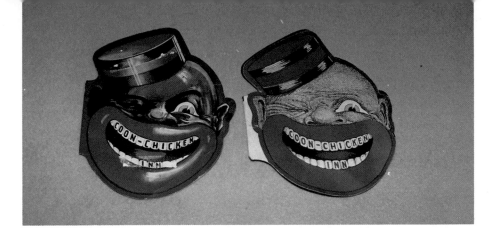

Coon Chicken Inn menus. 8½". 1930-45.
$150-175 each.

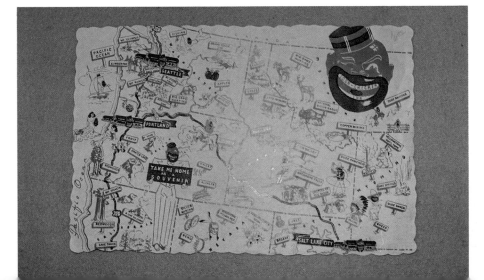

Linen post card from Coon Chicken Inn
Restaurants, showing the restaurant and its
locations. 1930-40s. $25-30.

Coon Chicken Inn paper place mat. 10½" x
14½". 1920-40s. $25-40.

Match book from Sambo's restaurants. 1940-50s. $20-25.

Wooden tokens from Sambo's restaurant. Good for a free cup of coffee. 1950-60s. $5-7 each.

Board for cutting out the Coon Chicken Inn menus. 6½" x 8". $450-500.

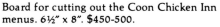

Laminated menu from Sambo's restaurant. 1950-60s. $30-40.

Stuffed tiger from Sambo's restaurant. "Sambo's tag along." 7". 1950-60s. $20-25.

Thermos from Sambo's restaurant. 1960-70s. $35-40.

Plate from Aunt Jemima kitchens. 10". 1940-50s. $65-85.

Plate from Sambo's restaurant. 10". "Jackson's China, Falls Creek, Pa." 1945-70. $125-150.

Souvenir glass from "Aunt Fanny's Cabin. Smyrna, Ga." 1970-80s. $22-25.

Mammy sticker from "Gerard's Chicken Inn,"
Salt Lake City, Utah. 5" x 4½". 1940-50s.
$40-50.

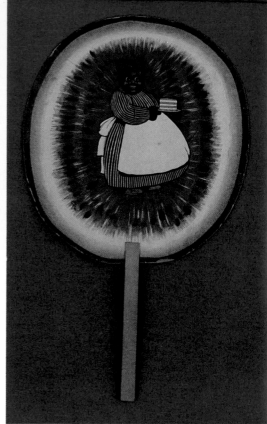

Cardboard fan from Mammy's Kitchen.
1930s. $125-150.

Ashtray from Smokquee restaurants.
"Garden City, Idaho." 1940-60s.
$40-45.

Cereal bowl from railroad, "Cream
of Wheat, 20th Century." 6½".
1920-30s. $165-185.

2
Banks

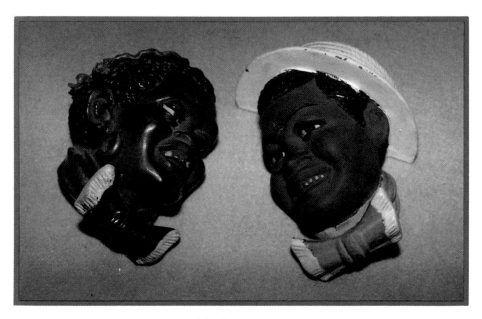

Minstrel wall banks. Terra cotta, 7". 1950s.
$85-100 pair.

Lady's head, bisque bank. "Japan." 5". 1920-
30s. $300-325.

Man's head, majolica bank. 4" x 2". 1920-40s.
$400-450.

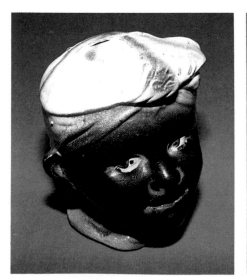

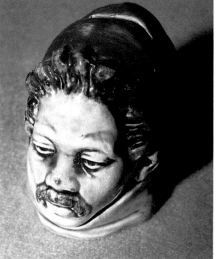

Native boy bobber standing by an orange which is a bank. Plaster, 1950s. $45-60.

Native boy bobber sitting on melon that is a bank. Plaster. $45-60.

Cast aluminum "Jolly Nigger" bank. Starkies, foreign. 7". When a penny is put in his hand he puts it in his mouth and his eyes close. 1900-1920s. $350-400.

Cast iron bank. "Jolly Nigger, Shepard Hardware Co. Buff. N.Y." 7". When a penny is placed on the hand, he puts it in his mouth and his eyes close. c. 1882. $450-500.

Cast iron bank with a man in doorway of cabin. Put a penny on the roof and he kicks it into the cabin. 3½". Circa 1875. $475-550.

Rare pottery bank of a native boy stirring a pot. 5" x 4". 1940-50s. $75-95.

Cast iron mammy bank. 5¼". 1930s. $125-140.

Plaster bank with mammy bathing her babies. 6½". Marked "Conovers orig." 1945. $65-75.

Mammy with basket, pot metal bank. 1935-45. $85-100.

25

3
Barware

Set of 5 glasses with band players. 3". 1930s.
$120-150 set.

Bust of man tankard. Ceramic. 1920s. 7".
$250-275.

Bottle stopper of man in top hat. Wood, 4".
1920s. $50-75.

Rare serving tray featuring Josephine Baker. 12". $350-400.

Bottle stopper of man's head. Marked: "Ceramic, Germany." 3". 1940s. $25-50.

Coaster set. It holds eight coasters in a box. "Jerywil Prods." $50-60.

Large mouth man, nut cracker. Brass. 4". 1930s. $275-300.

Ceramic drummer decanter. "Cebello Sherry-Jerey." Italy, 1950s. 11". $75-100.

Decanter of waiter. Baccarat. Satin glass with amethyst head. 1890s. $350-400.

Book with several stories. One is "Little Black Sambo." 1937. $95-110.

The Ten Little Nigger Boys: The Stump Book. Hard back with cardboard pages. 1910-1920s. $175-200.

"Ten Little Niggers" in a German translation. $95-125.

Minstrel Songs Old and New, Oliver Ditson and Co. 9" x 11½". 1870s. $55-65.

Music script, "Little Black Sambo" book. "Musette Publishers," 1942. 10" x 10". 1947. $45-55.

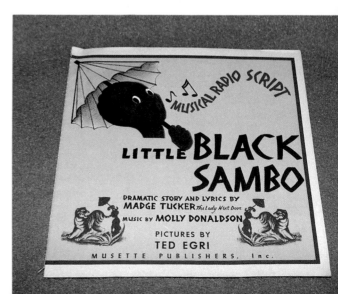

5
Bottle Openers

Brass clown bottle opener. 4½". 1920s.
$250-300.

Wall-mounted, cast iron bottle opener. 4".
1940-50s. $125-145.

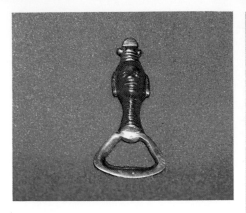

Brass native bottle opener. 4″. 1940-50s.
$15-20.

Pot metal native bottle opener, with
rhinestone eyes. 4½″. 1940-50s. $25-30.

Pot metal native bottle opener, with
rhinestone eyes. 5½″. 1940-50s. $40-50.

Pot metal native bottle opener, with
rhinestone eyes. 4½″. 1940-50s. $30-40.

Cast iron native bottle opener and paper
weight. 4½″ 1940-50s. $35-40.

6
Clocks

Cast iron banjo man clock. 15¼". 1970-80s.
$150-175.

Wooden wall clock with a boy holding a golliwog doll. "Germany." 7½" x 4". 1920-30s. $160-190.

Pressed wood man's face clock. The tie swings back and forth. 1940-50s. $175-200.

Wooden advertising clock for "Trixie Molasses." Lead weights. 1930-40s. $165-190.

Clock made by the Lux Clock Co. Waterbury, Conn. When wound, the boy's arms move up and down polishing the lady's shoes. 4". 1940s. $325-375.

Wind-up table clock, made by "Lux Clock Co.,
Waterbury, Conn." Two children sitting;
alligators are the hands of the clock. 1935. 4".
$300-350.

Mammy clock, pot metal. Full figure with
bow in hair. $675-750.

7
Figures

Metal

Bronze figure lying on ivory, smoking cigarette. 3". $385-425.

Metal figurine of boy and girl sitting on a stump. 3". $95-120.

Lead girl holding baby with cat behind him. 1½". 1910. $125-150.

Lead Fgures holding umbrella. 2½". 1920s. $175-200.

Lead bobber musician. 2". Early 1900s. $200-225.

Lead figure holding fishing pole. 3". 1920s.
$175-200.

Amos and Andy figurine. Metal, 4½". 1930s.
$200-250.

Bronze grouping of man and woman having
tea. 1½". $250-275.

Brass figurine of two men leaning over a real
piece of ivory. 3" x 5". 1930s. $250-300.

Comic character figure. Metal. 1915.
$200-225.

Pewter figurine of lady with baby. 2½".
1920s. $200-225.

Figurine of Johnnie Griffin made of metal.
4½". Early 1900s. $200-250,

Bronze slave in
chains. "L Kley."
5⅜". Late 1800s.
$250-275.

Figurine of baby with pig. Silver on pewter.
2". Early 1900s. $275-300.

Lead figures of two men with an alligator on sea shell. 4". 1920s. $250-275.

Cast iron mammy with basket on her head, soap dish. 5¼". 1930s. $425-450.

Lead figure of man with donkey. 2". 1920s. $225-250.

Cast iron figurine of three natives in a boat.
4". 1930s. $65-75.

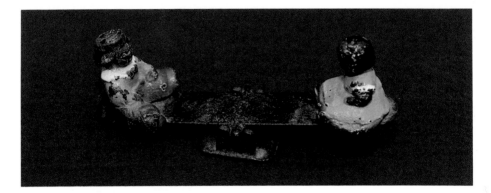

Children on a teeter totter. Cast iron, 5" x 2".
1915-25. $125-150.

Three lead figurines. 4". 1910-20s. $325-350
set.

Wax

Three wax figurines on base. 8″ tall. Late
1800s. $2000-2500.

Right: Wax figure of a woman with a basket of vegetables. "Vargas." $250-300.
Middle: Figurine of wax "Vargas" lady. Arms missing. 7″. 1930s. $125-145. Left:
Wax figurine of a man with an alligator on a rope. "Vargas." $250-300.

Majolica

Majolica boy lying down eating melon. 7" x 4". 1920-30s. $375-400.

Majolica figurine of a boy near flowers. "#52." 11½". 1920-30s. $275-300.

Majolica figurine of a lady lying down with her hand on her chin. 6½" x 3½". 1920-40s. $350-375.

Majolica figurine of girl sitting playing banjo. 1920-30s. $600-650.

Majolica figurine of a boy with his hand to his face. 1920-30s. $575-625.

Majolica figurine of a boy with a sack on his shoulder. 7" x 2½". 1920-30s. $400-425.

Other Ceramics

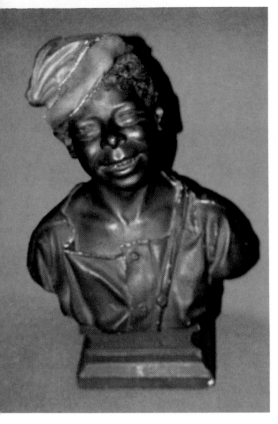

Bisque figurine of choir singers. 5" x 6". 1940-50s. $45-60.

Plaster statue of Civil War boy, "The Nation's Ward." Posed by Edward V. Valintine, of Richmond, Virginia. 24½". $1,200-1,500.

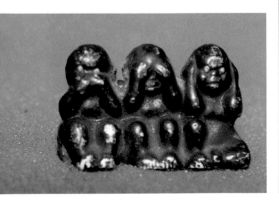

"See no evil, hear no evil, speak no evil." Three little boys in bisque. "Japan." 1½". 1920s. $40-45.

Plaster bust of a Civil War child. 18". $400-450.

Bisque figurine of a baby holding a pot. Early
1900s. $145-170.

Bisque figurine of a boy on a potty, wearing a
top hat. 1890s. $65-75.

Ceramic figurine of a little girl praying, 3".
1980s. $15-20.

Little boy with dog figurine. "Black is
beautiful." 1980s. $10-15.

Bisque figurine of boys sitting on a sofa eating cake. "Germany." 4" x 5". 1920-30s. $145-160.

Bisque figures of children near potty. 3". 1920s. $150-175.

Bisque figure of two little girls hugging. "Germany". 4". Early 1900s. $150-175.

Bisque figurines of a boy and girl sitting on a bench. 4". 1950s. $55-65 pair.

Staffordshire china figurine, "Uncle Tom's Cabin." 6½". Late 1800s. $500-600.

Staffordshire china figurine, Uncle Tom and Eva. 11". Late 1800s. $600-650.

Staffordshire china figurine, Uncle Tom and Eva. 8". Late 1800s. $700-750.

Pottery figurine of a native under an umbrella. 5½". 1940s. $40-45.

Bisque figure of man sitting in chair. 6" 1920s. $175-200.

Bisque little boy sitting on bale of cotton eating melon. 3". 1930s. $45-65.

Bisque minstrel figure on chair. 6". 1920s. $150-200.

Bisque figurine of a boy playing an accordion. "Japan." 5". 1940s. $125-140.

Bisque figure of man. 5". 1920s. $125-15

Bisque figure of a banjo man. 3¾.". 1920s. $125-150.

China figurine. 6". 1920s. $175-200

Ceramic figurine of a boy with a dancing cane. "Occ. Japan." 5". 1940-50s. $45-55.

Bisque figurine of musician. "Occ. Japan." 3". 1940-50s. $45-50.

Little boy on potty eating watermelon. Bisque. 5". $85-125.

Ceramic figurine of a native. "Japan." 5". 1950s. $15-20.

Ceramic figurine of a little girl holding a water pot. 4". 1950s. $18-22.

Little girl on pot. Bisque. "Germany." 4½". 1930s. $45-55.

Bisque figure of minstrel man. 3½". 1920s. $125-150.

China Figure of "Jim" from "Huckleberry Finn." Marked: "Sebastian. Hudson, Mass." 3". 1948. $125-150.

Bisque figure of man. "Germany." 4". 1910. $125-150.

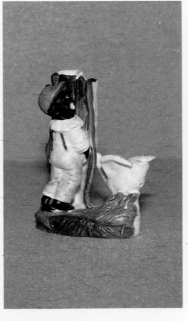

Ceramic figurine of shoeshine boy. "Occ. Japan." 6". 1940-50s. $65-85.

Bisque figurine of boy with goose, "Early bird catches the worm." "Japan." 2¾". 1940s. $40-45.

Ceramic figurine of a little boy. "Sambo." "Japan." $35-40.

Three musician figurines. China. 4". 1920s.
$300-350 set.

Chalk statue of Al Jolson, on his knees
singing "Mammy." 1940s. $125-150.

Musician figurine "Three cool cats". "Morro,
Hy De Ho". 1940s. $250-275.

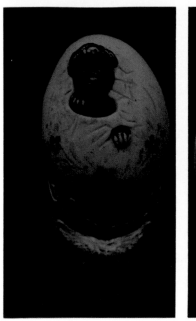
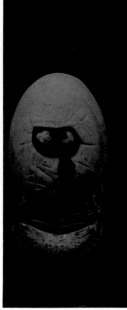

Bisque egg figurine with baby hatching from front and rear. 2". 1920s. $125-150.

Figurine of a baby coming out of a bisque egg, on a glass stand. 3". 1920-30s. $140-160.

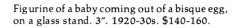

Shearwater woman with child. Pottery, 3". 1991. $60-75.

Man playing an accordion. Pottery, 3". "Shearwater 1990." $45-60.

Pottery figurine of Calypso girl playing the bongos. "Kreiss." 5½". 1940-50s. $40-50.

Set of five pottery figurines. "Japan." 4" x 1". 1940s. $125-140 set.

Bisque bobber figurines of a girl and boy. The boy is surprised at the naked girl who is holding her panties. 2½" x 5½". 1950s. $80-100 pair.

Bisque boy figurine sitting on melon. 4". 1915. $70-90.

Bobber Afro boy on cotton bale. Papier mâché, 7" x 2". 1930-40s. $65-80.

Bobber figurine of native boy holding fruit. Plaster, 1950s. $45-60.

Ceramic figurine of a boy holding a chicken. "Japan." 5". 1930-40s. $50-60.

Figurine of baby girl on a cloud, holding a washboard, with a clothes pin holding a halo in her hair. 4" x 4½". 1940s. $45-60.

Ceramic Santa figurine. 5".
1930s. $ 65-80.

Pottery figurines of boy and girl. 6". 1950s.
$60-75 pair.

Bisque boy eating melon. "Occupied Japan."
2½". 1940s. $75-100.

Souvenir of ceramic baby on cotton bale
eating melon. 1950s. $50-60.

Pottery figurine of a boy on the potty.
"Japan." 3". 1930s. $35-45.

Paperweight snow ball with babies on top of each other. 1920s. $95-125.

A man on the potty ceramic figurine. 6".
$65-85.

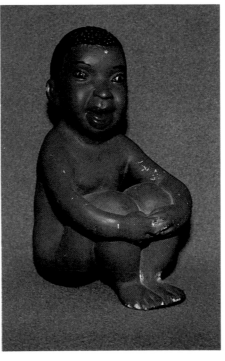

Paperweight snow flake ball with a boy eating melon. Glass bottom and ball. 3½" x 2½". 1920s. $225-250.

Seated boy of plaster. 1920s, 9½" high. $200-225.

Bisque incense burner of boy with faces on his feet. "Germany." 6". $85-100.

China figurine of mammy from New Orleans (repainted). 4". 1950s. $25-30.

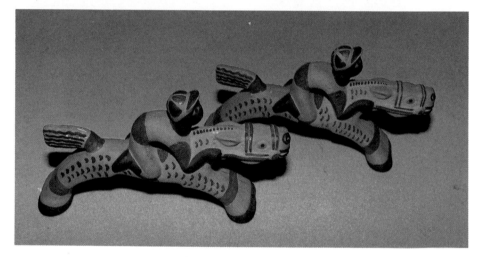

Pottery figurines of jockeys on horses. 6½" x4½". 1930s. $125-150 pair.

Army men playing dice. Ceramic, 3¾" x 6". 1940s. $175-225 set.

Set of bisque choir boys. 5". $125-150.

China Christmas figurines. Norel girl and
boy. 4½" x 3½". 1950s. $25-30.

Set of 6 ceramic children figurines. 6". 1940s.
$250-300 set.

Bisque figurine of three band players. "Occ.
Japan." 2" x 1½". 1940s. $60-70.

Pair of pottery
native man and
woman figurines.
10" x 6½". 1930s.
$160-200 pair.

Man riding a horse. Pottery, 4". "Shearwater 1990." $ 55-70.

Man carrying a bag of cotton. Pottery, 3". "Shearwater 1990." $55-70.

Bisque figurine of boy riding a pig. 4". Japan. $85-100.

Other Materials

Golliwog nurse, plastic figurine. "England." 1". 1940s. $15-20.

Rubber comic character figurine. 3". 1960s. $8-10.

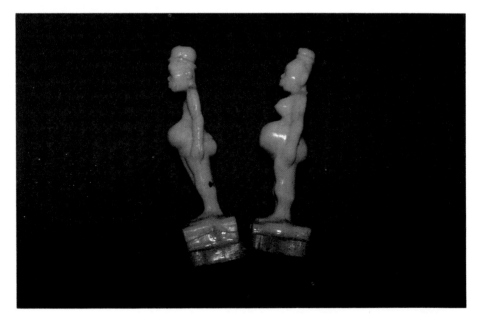

Plastic magnetic figurines of nude natives. 5". 1950s. $40-45.

Pressed wood man figure 5½".
1930s. $50-75.

Wooden yard figure of a little girl with
sprinkling can. 24". 1940-50s. $75-90.

Wooden figurine of a native girl and boy in
shells. 6". 1940s. $30-35.

8

Folk Art

Wooden folk art man, swinging his chain.
13". 1930-40s. $65-85.

Carved wooden folk art bust of a lady in a hat.
11". 1980s. $150-175.

Carved wooden folk art bust of a man
smoking a cigar. 9". 1980s. $125-140.

Folk art Banjo man and dancing mammy. Cardboard. 21″ x 18″. 1930s. $450-600 pair.

Folk art. Papier mâché banjo man, sitting in a melon car. Comes apart for use as a candy container. Composition head. 1980s. $350-400.

Carved wooden folk art mammy doll. 17".
1980s. $150-175.

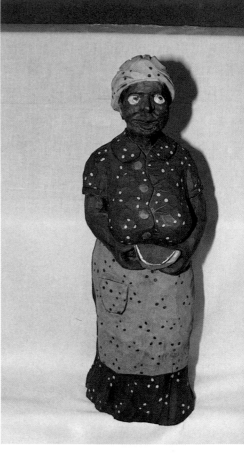

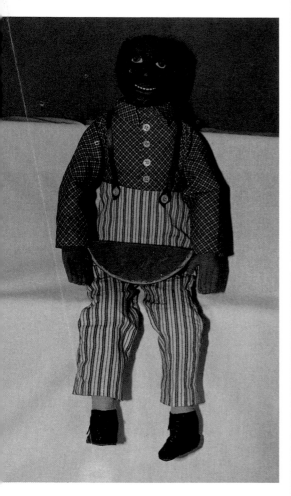

Folk art male doll with carved wooden head
and cloth-stuffed body. 22". 1980s. $145-160.

Male folk art doll with carved wooden head
and cloth-stuffed body. 16". 1980s. $125-145.

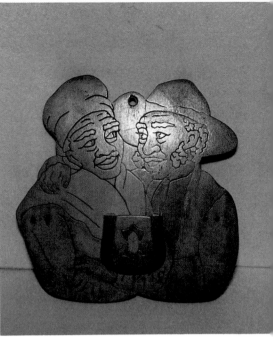

Lady's face wall hanging. Papier mâché. 8".
1920s. $300-350.

Folk art wooden match holder, wall hanger.
Mammy and friend, "Well matched."
$125-150.

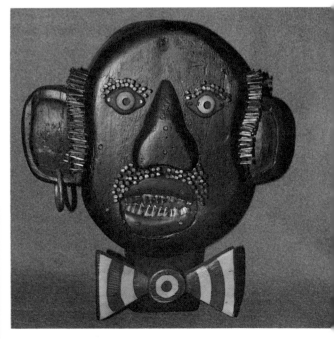

Folk art wooden wall-hanging. 6".
$60-80.

Wooden folk art. Nails for mustache and hair.
Real teeth. 15" x 13½". 1920-30s.
$1,200-1,500.

Folk art Jack-in-the-box. Wood box with papier mâché Golliwog figure. 13″. 1980s. $185-225.

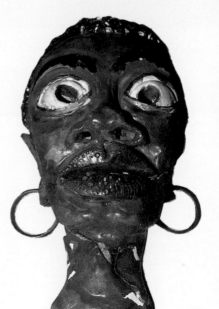

Folk art shoe shine stand. Approximately 3½′. 1920-30s. $3,500-4,000.

*This item was stolen from a shop in Mans Choice, Pa. There is a reward for the finder. Contact Police in that area.

Native head wall placque. Hand made pottery folk art. 5″ x 11″. 1920-30s. $80-100.

Hand-carved wood priest sitting in a chair.
11". Mid-1800s. Priceless piece of folk art.

Wooden man's head. Folk art. 15" x 23".
1920s. $300-350.

9

Greeting Cards

Greeting card. 3" x 5". 1940-50s. $4-5.

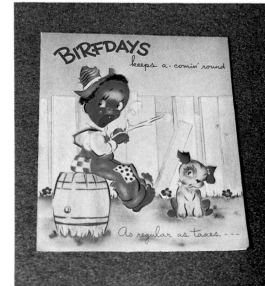

Greeting card. "Greetings, Inc." 5" x 6". 1942.
$5-6.

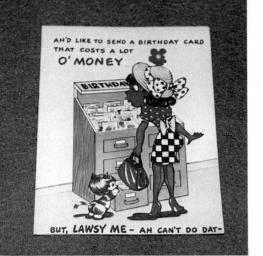

Greeting card. "Nova Laugh." 1952. 4½" x 6".
$6-7.

Greeting card. "DA Card Co." 4″ x 5¼″. 1940. $5-6.

Greeting card. "Hallmark." 5″ x 5″. 1945. $5-6.

Greeting card. "Doubl-Glo." 4½″ x 5″. $7-8.

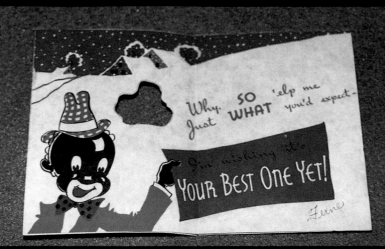

73

Greeting card with 10 little bisque babies. 1".
Early 1900s. $450-500.

Paper valentine. "Hall Bros." 6". $5-6.

Paper stand-up greeting card. Two children
on a pony with a Golliwog doll hanging on the
rocker. "Raphael Tuck Co." $45-70.

Greeting card. "Hallmark." 4" x 5¾". 1940s.
$5-6.

Picture of little girl. Oil. 5" x 7". 1920s. $125-150.

Cardboard picture of children, "Kiss me Rastus, nuthin makes me sick." 2½" x 7". 1930s. $18-22.

Plaster plaque of a smiling boy saying a poem. 1950s. $35-40.

Picture of a boy jumping out of the way of a bowling ball. Pressed fiber board. 1950s. $40-45.

Picture of two ladies, on silk. 14" x 10". 1880s-1900. $175-200.

Tin photograph of a lady with a big smile. 10" x 12". 1930s. $90-125.

Photo-post card of white smiling baby and black crying baby. "Cook Co., Ft. Smith, Ark" 6½" x 4½". 1920s. $35-45.

Wooden slave yolk.
From Henry Cason
and Bill Yober,
Wamego, Kansas.
40". $1,800-2,200.
(Photo of them in
later years.)

Decal with boy run-
ning carrying a
melon. 4½" x 6".
1950s. $15-20.

Picture of two couples strutting down the street. Embroidery on cotton. 17" x 10". Early 1900. $225-250.

Picture of wooden cabin with boy and melon and wood melon in corner. 1909. 8" x 12". "Yo all can hab de rine." $125-150.

Oil painting of a mammy on canvas. Signed, Marie Powell. 22" x 19". 1934. $900-1100.

11
Jewelry

Native women,
metal earrings.
1940s. $35-45.

Native women, plastic earrings. New. $15-20.

Native woman,
ceramic pin. 2" x 1".
1940. $30-40.

Cuff links of African masks. Inlaid porcelain.
1940-50s. $35-40.

Little Black Sambo steel-plated cuff links.
1940-50s. $30-40.

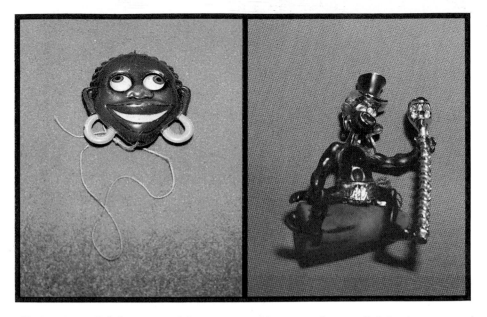

Native, tin pin. Pull the string and the eyes go back and forth. "Germany." 2½". 1930s. $40-50.

Native on a log, pin. Bakelite log, pot metal man. 1940-50s. $60-75.

Native winking eye children, plastic pins. 1950s. $25-30 pair.

Little Black Sambo steel-plated cuff links and tie bar. 1940-50s. $45-55 set.

Lighting

Plaster lamp with little boy holding a pineapple. "Japan." 1950s. $65-80.

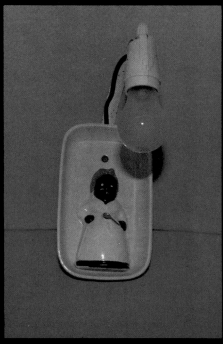

Ceramic wall lamp with mammy in center. $185-220.

Cast metal jockey table lamp with original paint. Electric. 19½". $325-350.

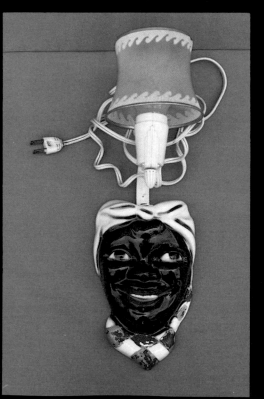

Ceramic mammy wall lamp. 1940s. $275-325.

Our Gang 16mm film, "Little Rascals." Hal Roach. 4" x 4". 1924. $35-45.

View Master reel. "Little Black Sambo." 1948. $10-15.

Our Gang 16mm film, "Cowboys and Indians." Hal Roach. 4" x 4". 1924. $35-45.

Castle Film's, "Little Black Sambo." 16mm, 4" x 4". $35-45.

14
Office and Desk Accessories

Man holding two ink wells. Bronze, 7". Early
1900s. $450-500.

Bronze paper weight. "Austria." 2¼" 1910.
$125-150.

Brass paperweight. Figure of native man.
4½". 1920s. $150-175.

Cast iron paper weights of a mammy and a butler. 1". 1930-40s. $90-100 each.

Cast iron pencil sharpener with the blade in the man's mouth. 1½". 1940s. $85-100.

Paper weight of a man on a fence, eating melon. 3". $145-170.

Pottery figurine of native. Pencil holder. "Japan." 5". 1950s. $35-40.

Mammy paperweights. Lead. 1920s. $150-250 each.

Wooden mammy pencil holder. It comes apart at the waist to hold pencils. 7". 1920-30s. $100-120.

Card holder with a man holding a basket for cards. Metal man on brass stand. $325-375.

Pot metal native card holder. "Black Magic." 12". 1930-40s. $140-160.

Letter opener of Johnnie Griffin. Solid brass. 12". Early 1900s. $375-450.

Thermometer on ivory with bronze holder of 3 natives around fence. 8". $350-425.

Plaster bookends with boy eating melon. 4½"
x 6". 1945-50s. $125-150.

Pressed wood book ends of men playing
guitars. 5" x 8". $1940s. $125-150.

Brass ink well of Johnnie Griffin.
6". $350-400.

15

Planters

Ceramic planters of boys playing instruments. "Occ. Japan." 1940-50s. $40-50 each.

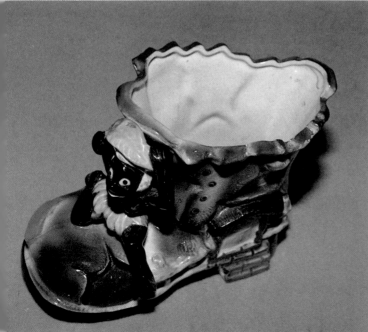

Shoe with native boy on top, ceramic planter. "Japan." 5½" x 6½". 1950s. $60-85.

Majolica planter of boy sitting on stump. 8″.
1920s. $475-500.

Ceramic planter of
a native boy in a
boat. "Japan." 6½″ x
5″. 1940s. $45-55.

Banana boat ceramic
planter by McCoy
Pottery Co. 10½″ x
5½″. 1930s. $65-90.

Ceramic planter with a native lady on a tiger's back. "Japan." 9" x 7". 1940s. $60-80.

Band player, planter. "Japan." 6" x 4½". 1930-40s. $95-125.

Ceramic planter of a native lying on a log. "Japan." 1950s. $40-50.

Man's head planter. Ceramic, 4". 1940-50s. $50-75.

Butler, rare ceramic planter. "Japan." 4½" x 4". 1930-40s. $190-225.

Repainted ceramic baby face planter. "Japan." 8". 1950s. $25-30.

Boy eating melon, ceramic planter. "Japan." 5½". 1950s. $45-55.

Pottery planters of a native boy and girl. 3".
1960s. $35-40 pair.

Native, ceramic planter. "Japan."
1940-50s. $35-45.

Mammy holding basket, pottery planter.
1950s. $65-80.

Bisque planter of a baby eating a piece of
melon. 4". 1940s. $45-60.

16

Plates

Three plates with "Brownie Downing." 4".
1920s. $200-225.

Butter pat mammy. Marked: "hand painted
by Web." 3". 1930s. $75-100.

Calendar plate with a boy eating melon. 7½". 1915. $125-160.

Plate from the Holiday Inn. "Vera Holiday sitting at a typewriter." 1980s. $55-65.

Mammy plate. Marked "Semi porcelain." 6". 1920s. $125-150.

China plate with music on the front.
"Fonderville, N.Y." 6½". $70-85.

China plate. "Prayer time at Uncle Tom's
cabin." Early 1900s. $75-100.

Souvenir China plate with painting of a boy riding an alligator. "Florida." 1930-40s. $125-150.

Plate with a painting of a little girl eating melon. 1930s. $65-75.

China plate with natives on front. "Japan." 10½". 1950s. $45-55.

17

Playing Cards

Deck of "Old Maid" cards with Steppin' Sam.
"W.P Co." 4" x 2". 1950s. $50-60.

Deck of cards. "Old Maid." 2½" x 3". 1940-
50s. $35-40.

Deck of regular playing cards with a picture on the back of a man and woman picking cotton. 4" x 2". 1940-50s. $45-60.

Deck of "Old Maid" playing cards. 2½" x 4". 1940-50s. $45-60.

Double deck of regular advertising playing cards, with a picture of a butler with a house on a tray. "Have one on the house, Tamko Roof." 4" x 2". 1950-60s. $70-80.

"Ole Maid" playing cards with Sambo card. 2½" x 4". 1940-50s. $35-40.

Record by Louis Armstrong "The Night Before Christmas." Feb. 26, 1971. $12-15.

"Little Black Sambo" record and book. $75-85.

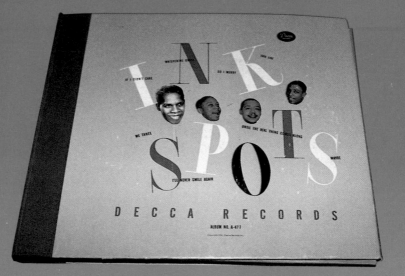

Record album, "The Ink Spots." 4 records. 1946. $30-40.

Record, "Basin Street Blues." 1940s. $60-75.

Record album. "The Birth of the Blues." Lena Horn, soloist. 1920-30s. $35-50.

Recod: "Oh Susanna.'' "Voco Co.
U.S.A." 7". 1948. $60-80.

Record of "Shoo Fly Pie and Apple Pan
Dowdy." $85-95.

Wooden dancing man for atop a record player
arm. 8". 1930-40s. $130-160.

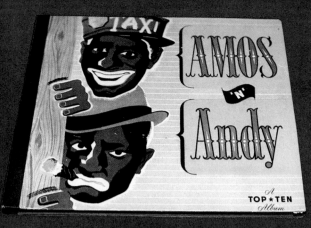

Record album, "Amos 'N' Andy." 4 records. 1928. $45-55.

Record album, "Al Jolson." 4 records. 1949. $30-40.

Record album "Jolson Sings Again." 4 records. 1949. $35-40.

103

19

Sewing Goods

Little girl, handmade wooden thread holder.
1960s. $20-25.

Boy playing dice, bisque pin cushion. "Japan."
3". 1940s. $65-75.

Tape measure in little girl's head. Celluloid,
1¾". 1940s. $125-150.

Little girl, wooden handmade thread holder.
1960s. $20-25.

Mammy pin cushion. 3". 1930-40s. $45-55.

Mammy pin cushion with cloth body and wood head. 5". 1945-50. $40-45.

Ceramic figure of man sitting, with a pin cushion in his hat. "Japan." 3". 1940-50s. $40-45.

Bisque native baby with bottle in its mouth and a melon that is a pin cushion. "Japan." 2½" x 3". 1940s. $140-160.

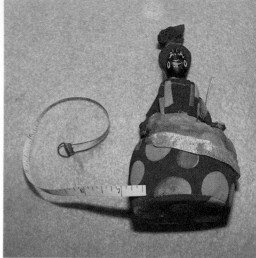

Pot metal pin cushion with tape measure in hat. "Germany." 1½". 1930s. $145-160.

Mammy pin cushion and tape measure, with wooden head and cloth body. 5". 1940-50s. $55-65.

Celluloid dancing man tape measure. 4". $125-150.

Celluloid man's head tape measure. 1½". 1920s. $175-200.

20

Smoking Accessories

Cigarette and Match Holders

Majolica match and cigarette holder. Boy with melon. 1920s. 7". $450-500.

Majolica cigarette and match holder. Boy sitting on fence. 7". 1920-40s. $350-400.

Boy on cotton, pot metal cigarette holder and ashtray. "England." Late 1800s. $375-425.

Bust of boy with crooked hat, match holder. Plaster, 7". 1930-40s. $185-225.

Pottery match holder of mammy with umbrella. 5". 1930s. $55-65.

Full-figure chef, chalk match holder. 5". 1940s. $65-75.

Majolica boy match and cigarette holder. 1920-40s. $350-375.

Bellhop cigarette and match holder. Brass with wood head. 1940-50s. $65-75.

Cigarette and match holder. Metal woman with baskets on brass stand. $350-400.

Match holder of man with mouth open. China, 4". 1930s. $35-40.

Bisque match holder with a baby coming out of an egg and a rooster sitting by him. 4". 1930s. $80-100.

Tooth pick or match holder with two boys near a cotton bale. Pot metal. $125-150.

Sculpted metal native figurines. The drummer is a match holder, the dancer is a match striker, and the bongo player is a lighter. 4½" each. 1930-40s. $150-180 set.

Majolica match and cigarette holder. Boy holding basket. 6½". $450-500.

Majolica cigarette and match holder. Boy sitting by boxes. 7". 1920-40s. $375-425.

Man match holder. 2¾". 1920s. $125-150.

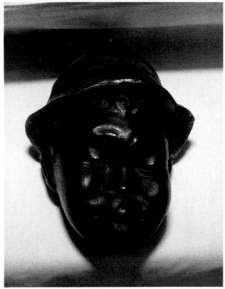

Johnnie Griffin-type plaster match holder. 6". 1930-40s. $125-145.

Lead figure of a boy on a horse getting water from a well. Match and cigarette holder. 9½". 1910. $850-1,000.

Man smoking cigarette near basket, match holder. Bronze, 1920s. $250-275.

White metal man with basket cigarette holder. 5". 1920s. $200-250.

Rare bronze cigarette and match holder. Boy sitting on bales of cotton. Late 1880s. $575-650.

Boy with a pair of shoes match holder. Metal, 4". Early 1900s. $375-400.

Bisque cigarette and match holder with ashtray. Little babies in cotton bales. "Japan." 5" x 2". 1940s. $55-65.

Pot metal cigarette and match holder. 10½" x 7½". Late 1800s. $375-425.

Donkey pulling cart, China cigarette box. 6½" x 8". $85-95.

Brass cigarette dispenser. Bartender.
8". 1930s. $1,500-1,800.

Smokquee, ceramic cigar holder. "Japan." 8".
1940-50s. $85-100.

Cigarette dispenser. Wood-open door man
pops out with cigarette. 3" x 5". 1920s.
$150-175.

Ashtrays

Cast iron skillet, ashtray. "L.H.C. Japan." 1950s. $35-40.

Cast iron skillet, ashtray. "New Orleans." John Wright, foundry. 4½". 1940-50s. $35-35.

Cast iron skillet, ashtray. Mammy's head in tray. John Wright, foundry. 5¾" 1940-50s. $65-75.

Mammy, cast iron skillet ashtray. 4" x 3". 1930-40s. $125-150.

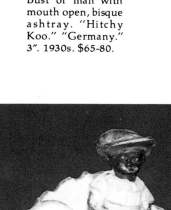

Boy climbing in pot, bisque ashtray. "Japan." 1940s. $35-40.

Bust of man with mouth open, bisque ashtray. "Hitchy Koo." "Germany." 3". 1930s. $65-80.

Bisque ashtray of little boy pushing a pot "Japan." 1½". 1930s. $25-30.

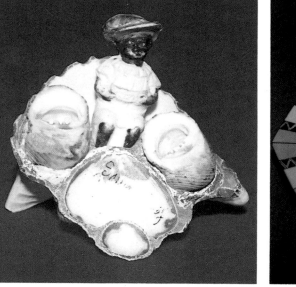

Bisque baby sitting in a shell ashtray. 1930-40s. $45-55.

Porcelain ashtray with picture in the center of a boy playing banjo. 1940s. $125-140.

Ceramic ashtray with boy holding alligator's mouth open. "Japan." 5". 1940-50s. $45-60.

Servant, China cigarette holder and ashtray. 7½" x 3½." 1935-40s. $150-200.

Golfer swinging, pottery ashtray. 6½" x 4". 1950s. $40-50.

Naughty goose, China ashtray. 3" x 2". 1950s. $35-45.

Ashtray with little boy on clothes line while dog sits holding his pants in its mouth. Bisque, 3½". 1940s. $35-40.

Plaster ashtray with mammy stuck in the wringer. "Oh my aching back." 6". 1950s. $45-50.

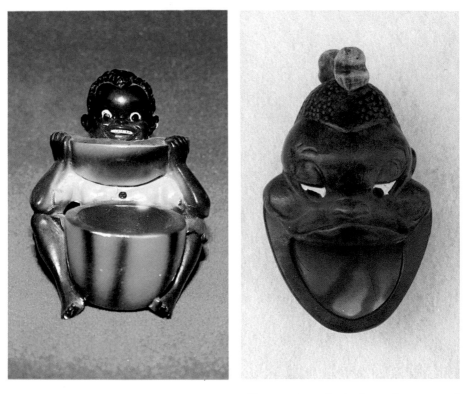

Ashtray with boy eating melon. Plaster, 5¾". 1950s. $45-55.

Pottery ashtray in the form of a native with an open mouth. "Japan." 1950s. $35-40.

Painting of baby on ashtray. "Noritaki." 5".
1940s. $70-90.

Ashtray of derogatory man's
head. China, 4". 1930s. $45-60

Bisque ashtray, cigarette holder. Man playing
horn. "Japan." 4" x 2½". 1950s. $40-50.

Boy playing dice, bisque ashtray. 2½" x 2".
1950s. $35-40.

"Evening exercise." Girl on swing near fence, rare China ashtray. 3" x 4". 1930-40s. $100-125

Pair of China ashtrays with baby crawling in center. 5" and 3". 1930s. $160-200 pair.

Ashtray of pot metal. Boy on bench eating melon. 1930s. $45-55.

Ceramic ashtray with boy pulling a cart. "Japan." 4". 1940s. $30-35.

Boy on pot with bee, bisque ashtray. "Japan." 3" x 3". 1930s. $30-35.

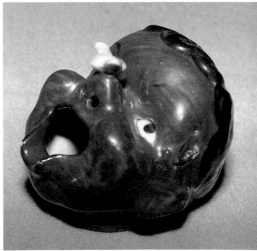

Man with bee on nose, ceramic ashtray. "Japan." 3" x 2". 1950s. $35-40.

Boy with cigar in mouth, brass bobber ashtray. 5". $150-175.

Boy holding onto dice, bisque ashtray. "Japan." 3" x 3". 1950s. $40-45.

Man playing horn, ashtray and cigarette holder. Souvenir of Tampa, Florida. "Japan." 4½" x 2½". 1950s. $40-50.

Brass ash tray, boy with large hat. 4½". 1920s. $175-200.

German ashtray. China, 7½". $40-50.

Lighters

Cigarette lighter. Horn player embossed of front. 1920s. $110-140.

Metal golfer, from a lighter (missing lighter). 6½". $50-60.

Rare bartender cigarette lighter and holder by "Ronson U.S.A." 6" x 7". $900-1100.

Humidors

Majolica humidor with boy lying on lid. 5½" x
8½". 1920-30s.
"#88." $350-400.

Top to humidor. Man lying on top of melon.
Pottery, 5" x 6". Late 1800s. $125-150. Top
only.

Top to humidor. Boy sitting on tobacco leaf.
China, iridescent. 4½" x 6". 1920-30s. $65-80.
Top only.

Humidor with boy's head as lid. Terra cotta,
5" x 7½". 1900-1920s. $550-650.

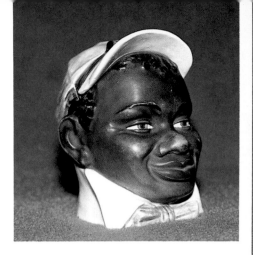

Boy's bust, majolica humidor. 5½". "Germany." 1920s. $350-400.

Man with removable hat, "Majolica" humidor, #1447-83. 6¾". 1930s. $300-325.

Bust of man smoking cigar, majolica humidor. 7". 1920-30s. $425-450.

Man with removable hat. "Majolica" humidor, #1371-28. 11½". 1930s. $475-550.

Majolica humidor. 6". 1920s. $400-450.

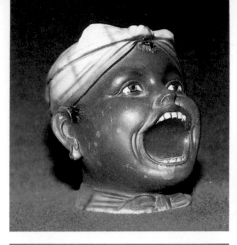

Lady's head with mouth wide open, porcelain humidor. 5½".
"Germany." 1900-20s. $400-450.

Man smoking pipe, porcelain humidor. "Germany." 1900-1920s. $400-450.

Bisque humidor of boy with a hat and bow tie. 1910-20s. $425-460.

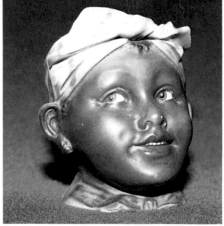

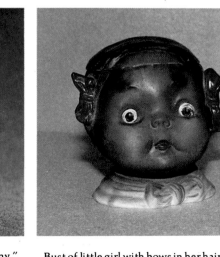

Lady's bust, porcelain humidor. "Germany." 1900-1920s. $400-450.

Bust of little girl with bows in her hair, bisque humidor. 4¾". 1920-30s. $425-460.

Pipes

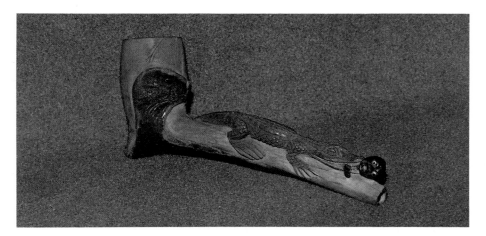

Wooden pipe. Alligator with boy's head in its mouth. 9". 1920s. $150-175.

Clay pipe, with natives' heads on bowl and handle. 7". 1930-40s. $125-150.

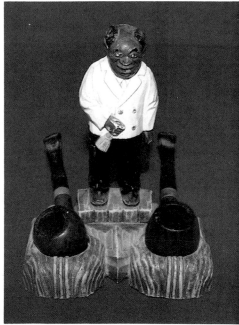

Butler, holder for pipes. Pressed wood. 1935-50s. $150-175.

21
Spoons

Sterling spoon. "Alabama." 1920s. $150-175.

Sterling spoon. Boy's head attached to melon. Marked "New Orleans" in bowl. 1920s. $150-175.

Sterling spoon with boy eating melon on handle, also mammy with basket of cotton on her head. Enamel. "Cinn., Ohio" in bowl. $200-250.

Sterling demi-spoon. Boy with cotton on handle and "Washington, D.C." in bowl. 1900-30s. $85-100.

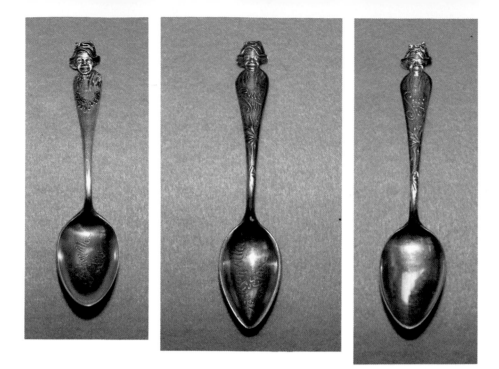

Top left: Souvenir sterling teaspoon. "Johnnie Griffin." "Sunny South" on handle, "Jackson, Fl." in bowl. "Greenleaf & Crosby" on back. $125-150.

Top middle: Souvenir sterling narrow bowl teaspoon. "Johnnie Griffin" and "Sunny South" on handle, and "Jacksonville, Fl." in bowl. "Greenleaf & Crosby" on back. $135-150.

Top right: Souvenir sterling teaspoon. "Johnnie Griffin" and "Sunny South" on handle. Plain bowl. $100-125.

Bottom left: Souvenir sterling teaspoon. Boy with big smile and hat on handle. "P.B." Plain bowl. $125-140.

Bottom right: Souvenir sterling teaspoon. Boy wearing a hat with corn on the handle. "Lookout Mountain" in bowl. $125-150.

Sterling spoon with boy's head on handle and cotton in bowl. 1920s. $145-175.

Souvenir sterling demi-spoon. Boy with hat, "Sunny South" and corn on the handle. "Jacksonville, N.C." in bowl. Signed Dorothy on back. $100-125.

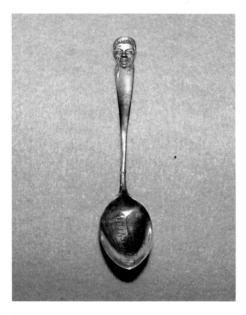

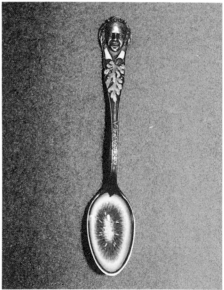

Souvenir sterling demi-spoon. Smiling boy with curly hair on handle. "Brandentown" in bowl. "A." on back. $120-140.

Sterling spoon with boy's head on handle and enamel melon in bowl. 1920s. $425-460.

22

Toys and Dolls

Tin wind-up native walker. 6". 1920-30s. $145-160.

Boy riding a turtle, tin wind-up toy in original box. "Japan." 1940-50s. $125-150.

Tin wind-up toy. "Amos and Andy Fresh Air Taxi," by Louis Marx. 5½" x 8". $1200-1500.

Tin wind-up little boy walker. 4½". 1920-30s. $350-380.

Strauss tin, mechanical, wind-up toy, "Ham and Sam." 7½" x 7" x 5". 1920s. $1,000-1,200.

Tin wind-up dancing man playing banjo on the roof. "Jazzbo Jim." "Unique Art Mfg. Co., Newark, N.J." 1921. 11". $900-1100.

Wind-up tin toy of native playing his drum. 6". 1930-40s. $150-175.

Tin wind-up dancing man on box. "Dapper Dan Coon Jigger." Louis Marx Co., May 24, 1910. 11". $850-1000.

"Be Bop, the Jivin' Jigger," tin wind-up toy.
10½". 1940-50s. $250-300.

Tin wind-up mammy. "Sweeping Mammy,"
by Linstrom. 8". 1920-30s. $225-240.

Tin wind-up dancing man with a celluloid
head. "Occ. Japan." 1940s. $225-260.

Wooden ink stamps. One is a minstrel man.
1920-30s. $125-145.

Child's game board. Back
side is checkers board.
"Noble & Noble N.Y."
12" x 12". 1929. $85-100.

Wood puzzle of Little
Black Sambo with tiger.
"Sifro." $80-100.

"Poor Jenny" game.
"Alderman and Fairchild
Co." 1927. $125-150.

"As You Like" puzzle. Five wood blocks. L.R. and Co. $125-150.

Game "The Bogie Man." "Globe Mfg. Co.," 1920-30s. $200-250.

Game of "Snakes and Ladders." "Globe Mfg. Co.," 1930s. $125-140.

This tin "Sambo" game came with suction cup darts and a gun. "Wyandotte Co." 22½" x 14". 1930-40s. $125-150.

Framed cardboard cutout of baby. 1940s. $70-80.

Checkered board with Bull Durham Advertising. Front, back, and rules on side. 14½" x 21½". June, 1880. $325-350.

Dancing man on a kazoo. "Japan." 11" x 17½".
1920-30s. $250-285.

Tin battery operated native drummer. "Line
Mar Toys, Japan." 10½". 1930-40s. $225-250.

Tin toy clackers with a man playing the
harmonica. 1935-40s. $25-30.

Figurine of a man playing the trumpet. 2½". 1950s. $35-40.

Tin tray with Golliwog inside. "England." 2". 1940s. $15-20.

Figurine of African woman with a basket on her head. 2". 1940s. $20-25.

Plastic figurine of Willie Mays. 1960s. $200-225.

Game of little boy with dice in a bubble on his head. Plastic, 2". 1930-40s. $125-150.

Wooden mammy walker toy. 4". 1935-50s. $45-60.

Coconut shell purses, with little girl faces. 4"
& 5". 1950s. $20-25.

Roly poly toy. Composition. 4". 1920s.
$175-200.

A doll on a drum pounding pegs in board,
used for a store display. The doll has been
painted and an electrical device added to
animate it. Put together in the 1950s. 2½ ft.
tall. $350-400.

Wind-up wooden rocking little girl, eyes go
back and forth. 10". 1920-30s. $250-275.

Wood Clacker toy. The boy's head pops out of barrel as it clacks. 4". $95-120.

Marionette in the box. Wood head, cloth body. 8". 1940s. $45-55.

Wooden game of dice. The dice fit in man's hat. Glass eyes. 2". 1920-30s. $85-100.

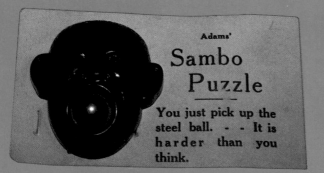

Sambo puzzle. Plastic, 2". 1935-45. $70-80.

Box of crayons with man's black face on box. 1950-60s. $15-20.

Little boy and girl paper dolls with clothes.
17". 1940-50s. $95-120.

Plastic bottle baby, with rubber nipple. 4".
1930-40s. $45-65.

Puppet. Composition. "Effenbee Lucifer."
13". 1920-30s. $250-300.

Papier mâché marionettes. 17". 1880-1900.
$250-300 each.

Wooden dancing native woman and paddle.
1940s. $85-110.

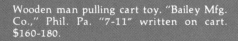

Wooden man pulling cart toy. "Bailey Mfg.
Co.," Phil. Pa. "7-11" written on cart.
$160-180.

"Mr. Bojangles" mobile in original package.
Plastic with top hat and bow tie. 1940-50s.
$45-60.

Mask made out of starched material. 1920s.
$85-100.

Mask made of wood. Late 1800s. $125-150.

Mask made out of papier mâché. Early 1900s.
$125-150.

Mask made out of papier mâché. Early 1900s.
$125-150.

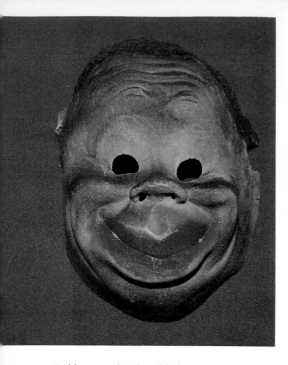

Rubber mask of a black man. 1940-50s. $65-75.

Wire fencing mask of black man with mustache. 12". 1910. $485-100.

Golliwog tin toy. Press the lever and the clown hits the Golliwog. "England." Early 1900s. $100-125.

Wooden dancing man. 10½". 1920s. $200-250.

Willie Mays nodder, composition, dated 1962. $275-300.

Bojangle jiggle toy. Made in U.S.A. 9". 1930s. $325-350.

Tin rattles. "Germany." 6". Early 1900s. $50-100 each.

Wooden game "Bean-O". 15" x 15". 1930s. $150-175.

Dolls

Corn husk mammy doll with nut head. 5". 1930s. $35-40.

Plastic baby doll. "Japan." 5". 1940-50. $20-25.

Cloth body doll with bisque head, arms, and legs. 10½". 1890. $300-350.

Pair of celluloid dolls with jointed arms and legs. 1½". 1930s. $90-120 pair.

"Frozen Charlotte"type miniature China baby. 1". 1930-40s. $20-25.

Celluloid bellboy. Carnival give away. 6½". 1920s. $85-100.

Papier mâché jointed doll. 6½". Early 1900s.
$225-250.

Nut head doll. 5". Early 1900s. $125-200.

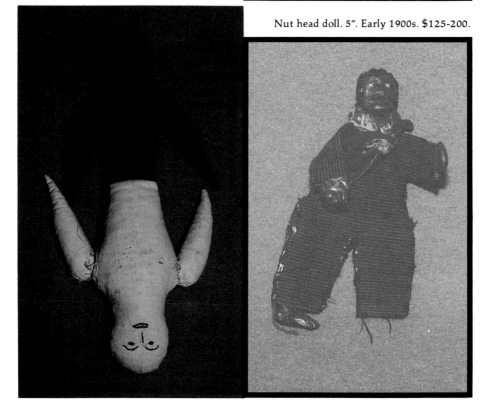

Straw-filled, topsy-turvy doll. Civil War era.
12". $250-290.

Composition figure, cloth body of man. Folk
art. 5". Early 1900s. $100-125.

Nut head doll, cloth body. 3½". Early 1900s.
$150-175.

Celluloid mammy doll with white baby. 4½".
1930s. $100-125.

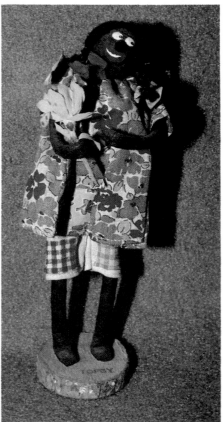

Little girl bisque doll. "Japan". 4½". 1920-30s.
$85-100.

Topsy doll with wooden head and wire body.
6½". 1930s. $150-175.

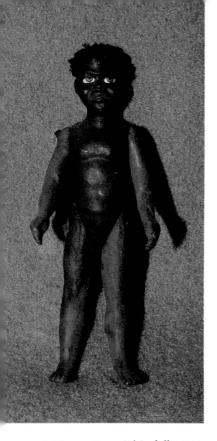

Cloth stuffed "Frederick Douglass" doll, in box. 1844. 8" x 11". Very Rare and Priceless.

Male papier mâché doll. 6½". 1920s. $250-300.

Papier mâché body and crepe paper clothes, mammy and butler dolls. 5½". Early 1900s. $250-300 pr.

All cotton mammy bell with no face. 4".
1940s. $25-30.

Pair of corn husk dolls, with nut heads.
1940s. 10". $70-90 pair.

Rag mammy doll with cotton stuffed body,
real hair, and sculpted face. 21". 1900s.
$325-350.

Folk art nut dolls. 7". 1900-1920s. $140-160.

Beloved Belindy rag doll. All original, cotton stuffed. 15". 1930s. $325-365.

Mammy holding baby, all cotton doorstop bottle. 10". 1920s. $125-150.

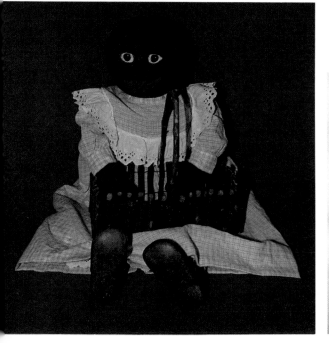

Folk art carved wooden baby doll. Cloth stuffed body, wooden head. 26". 1980s. $175-200.

Crochet doll, dress, and body. 9". 1940s. $35-40.

Mammy rag doll. All cotton with yarn hair. 5". 1940s. $35-40.

Golliwog rag doll with yarn hair and cloth stuffed body. 16". 1930s. $125-150.

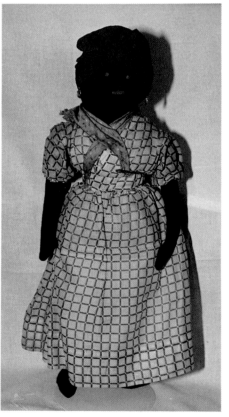

Palmera leaves mammy with baby, from New Orleans. 7". 1930s. $125-150.

Stuffed, jointed, all cotton rag doll, with original clothes and bandanna. Bead eyes. 15". 1940s. $85-100.

All cotton, jointed, stuffed rag doll, with yarn hair and sequin eyes. 7". 1920s. $50-65.

Cotton stuffed rag doll, with beaded eyes. 14". 1940s. $50-60.

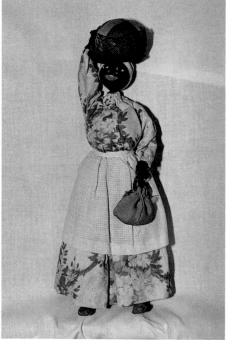

Nut head mammy doll with wire body. 7". 1940s. $35-40.

Stuffed "Norah Wellings" doll with original clothes. The doll is made of plush felt and wool hair, with glass eyes. 14". 1930s. $300-350.

Cotton stocking dolls with yarn hair, and dressed in old clothes. 12". 1930s. $40-50 each.

All cotton rag doll with yarn hair, and jointed arms and legs. 11". 1930s. $65-75.

Rag doll. Cotton stuffed, yarn hair. 8". 1950s. $18-22.

"The Pinn Famile", a family of five wooden dolls. Woodcraft Studios, Minn. 1950s. $145-170.

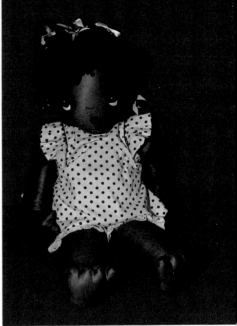

Little girl rag doll. Cotton stuffed, with jointed arms and legs. 21". 1920-30s. $95-125.

Rag doll with silk body, yarn hair, and jointed arms and legs. 14". 1930s. $65-80.

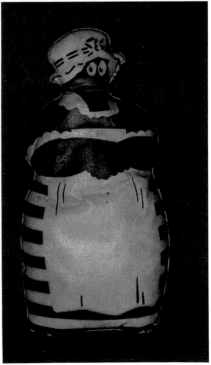

Jamaican doll with basket of fruit on her head. Plastic body with original clothes. 12". 1940s. $45-55.

"Rachel," oil cloth doll. 12". 1930s. $275-300.

23

Miscellaneous Memorabilia

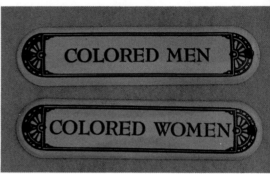

Enamel signs for colored men and colored women. 1940s. 10". $80-100 pair.

Black face choir boy wax candle, with hymnal. 3". 1940s. $25-30.

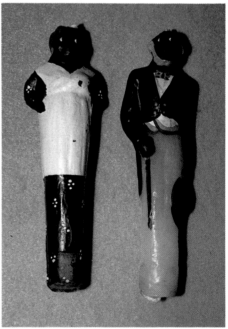

Boy sitting on log candy dish with lid. Pressed wood. 1940s. $85-100.

Mammy and butler candles. 5½". 1950s. $35-40 pair.

Candy dish made from a coconut shell, with a ceramic native girl. 8½" x 5". 1950s. $40-50.

Pot metal statue from the Ku Klux Klan, used to bring meetings to order. The arm comes off for transporting. $650-725.

K.K.K. brass token. "Member in good standing." 1¾". 1930–50s. $35-44.

Hand-blown glass Christmas tree ornament. 6¼". 1950s. $40–45.

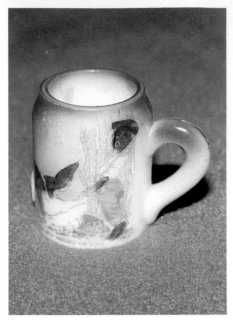

Souvenir tooth pick holder. Milk glass with a picture of a boy, near a fence with a naughty goose. 2¼". 1930s. $65-85.

After shave bottle, shaped like a man. 9½". One pint. 1935-40s. $125-150.

Boy with bucket, ceramic tooth pick holder. 3". 1950s. $25-30.

Man's head, China tooth pick holder. "Germany, C.D. Kenny." 3" x 1½". 1940s. $160-200.

Bisque tooth pick holder of a bobbing head little boy sitting. "Japan." 3". 1930-40s. $55-65.

Golliwog perfume bottle. Satin glass. 2½". 1920s. $100-125.

Political buttons. $5-6 each.

Pennant of a little girl. "Dis ain't no white trash." 1930s. $85-110.

Bibliography

Carson, Jeanette. *Black Ethnic Collectible Magazine,* Volume 4 No. 5, August, 1991. Hyattsville, Maryland.

Congdon-Martin, Douglas. *Images in Black: 150 Years of Black Collectibles.* West Chester, Pennsylvania: Schiffer Publishing Ltd. 1990.

Kader, Don. *Collectors' Showcase Magazine,* September-October, 1982, Vol. 2 No. 1. Los Angeles, California.

Morgan, Hal. *Symbols of America.* New York: Viking Penguin Inc., 1986.

Rainwater, Dorothy. *American Spoons Souvenir & Historical.* Pennsylvania: Thomas Nelson & Son & Everybody's Press, 1968.

Reno, Dawn E. *Collecting Black Americana.* New York: Crown Publishers Inc., 1986.

Smith, Darrell A. *Black Americana, A Personal Collection.* Minneapolis, Minnesota: Star Press, Inc., 1988.

Young, Jackie. *Black Collectibles: Mammy and Her Friends.* West Chester, Pennsylvania: Schiffer Publishing Ltd., 1988.

World Book Encyclopedia. 1991.

Mammy, plastic curtain pulls. 1½". 1950s.
$55-65 set.